MW00571354

Genre Realistic Fict'

Essential Question
What makes you laugh?

Funny Faces

by Elizabeth Brereton
illustrated by Caroline Romanet

Chapter 1
Missing Out

Max walked through the front door and went into the kitchen. "Hi, Mom, I'm home!"

"How was school, honey?" Mom asked.

"Great! I scored a goal in soccer!" said Max.

"Well done!" Mom passed Max his apple and a bowl of soup. "Would you mind taking this soup to Ella? She's got a bad cold."

Max took his apple and the bowl of chicken soup into the family room. Ella was sitting on the sofa with a blanket pulled up to her chin and tissues scattered around her. Her eyes were red and puffy.

"Here's your soup," Max said. He was about to leave, but then he heard Ella sniff. He turned around and realized that she was crying. "What's the matter?" he asked.

"I had to come home from school early," Ella said.

"That's not so bad. You can go back to school when you're feeling better," Max said, taking a bite of his apple.

"It *is* bad! I missed out on the zoo trip!" Ella said, sniffing again. "I haven't been to the zoo for ages." She looked very unhappy.

Max knew that Ella had been really looking forward to going to the zoo. For weeks, she had been talking about all the different animals her class would get to see.

Max chewed on his apple and thought. "Maybe I could make you feel better. I could be your entertainment instead of the animals at the zoo. I could make you laugh," he said.

Ella blew her nose and sat up a little. "How are you going to do that?" she asked.

STOP AND CHECK

Why was Ella upset?

Chapter 2
Try Again, Max

Max took another bite of his apple and thought for a while. What could he do to make Ella laugh? Suddenly, he had an idea. He stopped chewing his apple for a moment and sat down opposite Ella on the sofa.

"You couldn't go to the zoo today, but maybe I can bring the zoo to you," Max said. "Zoo animals make funny noises and funny faces. I can act them out for you!"

"Okay," Ella said, "I guess that could work."

For his first animal, Max decided to act like a lion. He made his hands into claws. "Roar!" he yelled, and then he lunged at Ella.

"That's not funny. That's scary!" Ella said, pulling the blanket back up to her chin.

"Sorry!" Max said, coaxing Ella out from under the blanket. "I'll try a different animal."

Max made his hands into a beak.

"What's that?" Ella asked.

"What's that?" Max repeated, moving his beak as he talked.

"Why are you copying me?" Ella asked.

"Why are you copying me?" Max repeated.

"Are you being a parrot?"

"Are you being a parrot?"

"That's not funny, Max! That's annoying!" Ella said, folding her arms across her chest.

Max sighed and dropped his hands. "Okay, I'll try again."

Max dropped to the living room floor and slithered across the carpet. "Sssss!" he said.

"You're being a snake," Ella said, "but there's nothing humorous about snakes."

Max sat back on the sofa and scratched his head. Making Ella laugh was harder than he'd thought it would be.

STOP AND CHECK

Why didn't Ella laugh at Max's animals?

Chapter 3
Monkey Business

"What am I doing wrong?" Max wondered out loud. He thought for a minute. "I know! I need to think of a funnier animal," he said.

"What about a monkey?" Ella suggested. "Monkeys are funny."

"Great idea!" Max said.

Max got off the sofa and crouched down. "Ooh-oooh! Ah-aah!" he said like a monkey.

Ella began to smile.

Max leaped up onto the sofa. "Ooh-oooh! Ah-aah!" he said. Then he began to scratch his armpits.

Ella started to giggle.

Mom poked her head around the corner to see what was happening. Max bounded over to her and pulled her into the room. Then he pretended to scratch her back. Soon, Mom was laughing her head off, too.

"Come here, silly monkey!" Mom said.

Max shook his head and disappeared into the kitchen. When he returned to the family room, he was eating a banana.

Max offered a banana to Ella. "Ooh-oooh? Ah-aah?" he asked.

"No, silly monkey! I don't want a banana!" Ella said, and she giggled again.

Max shrugged his shoulders and ate the rest of his banana while leaping around the room scratching his armpits. He had found the trick to making Ella laugh. All he had to do was be silly—the more ridiculous he looked, the better. Ella was smiling from ear to ear. Max jumped onto the sofa and tickled her.

"Monkeys can't tickle!" Ella said, in between giggles.

"I know, but I'm not a monkey anymore. I'm just Max!" Max said, and he laughed, too.

STOP AND CHECK

How did Max make Ella laugh?

Respond to Reading

Summarize

Use details from the story to help you summarize the important events in *Funny Faces*. Your chart may help you.

Details

↓

Point of View

Text Evidence

1. What kind of fiction is *Funny Faces*? Which details tell you this? GENRE

2. What does the narrator think about Max's efforts to make Ella laugh? Use details in the story to help you answer. POINT OF VIEW

3. What does the idiom "smiling from ear to ear" on page 14 mean? IDIOMS

4. Do you think Max does a good or bad job of trying to understand how Ella is feeling? Use details from the text to support your answer. WRITE ABOUT READING

Compare Texts

Read a funny poem about a surprise birthday gift.

My Cheeky Puppy

"Happy birthday," said Mom, giving me a box.
Was it a computer or a year's worth of socks?
But computers don't bark and socks don't kick.
The present jumped out and gave me a lick!

What should I name my lovable new pup?
I smiled as he wagged his tail and jumped up.
His eyes were bright and his coat was tip-top.
But look at those ears! I named him Flip Flop.

Illustration: Laura Ferraro Close

I opened more gifts—a book, a puzzle, a tie.
And while we were busy Flip passed us all by.
He went to the kitchen and made for the cake.
When time came to cut it we saw our mistake.

"We'll train him well! He'll learn to be good,"
I promised my mother, hoping that we could.
Mom stared at my puppy, all covered in drool.
"That dog needs to go to obedience school!"

The trainer looked sternly at crazy Flip Flop.
"I'll get him to sit still, to roll, and to drop!"
She whistled and yelled, but he wouldn't obey.
My Flip Flop ran in circles, and then ran away.

Sad and disheartened, with heads hanging
low, we decided to call it a day and just go.
I caught Flip Flop, leashed him, and then
We began walking home to tell Mom, when...

The Gray Street bullies jumped out of a tree!
They were older, tougher, and bigger than me
—nasty, naughty, mean through and through.
I shook and I trembled. Oh, what could I do?

Flip Flop to the rescue—that lovable pup!
He barked, growled, and chased them back up.
They stayed in the tree for the rest of the day.
And Flip Flop and I? We ran off to play!

Make Connections

What events does the author include in *My Cheeky Puppy* to make readers laugh? What made you laugh? ESSENTIAL QUESTION

Who is funnier, Max or the puppy? Explain your answer. TEXT TO TEXT

Focus on
Literary Elements

Rhyme Poetry is language that is arranged into patterns. Some poems rhyme. A poem that tells a story is called a narrative poem. Narrative poems often rhyme, because a rhyme pattern can give a poem a sense of moving forward.

Read and Find *My Cheeky Puppy* is a narrative poem written in rhyme. The words at the ends of the lines rhyme. Find the rhyming words, and then read the poem aloud to hear the rhymes clearly.

Your Turn

Write your own narrative poem about a pet. You can write about a real pet or you can make one up. Remember that a narrative poem tells a story. Make the words at the ends of some lines rhyme.